"THE WORLD'S EASIEST POCKET GUIDE"

— TO —

Making Your First College Decision

"THE WORLD'S EASIEST POCKET GUIDE"

TO

Making Your First College Decision

LARRY BURKETT

WITH KEVIN MILLER
ILLUSTRATED BY KEN SAVE

NORTHFIELD PUBLISHING

CHICAGO

Text & Illustrations © 2000 BURKETT & KIDS, LLC

Larry Burkett's Money Matters For Kids
Executive Producer: *Allen Burkett*

For Lightwave Publishing
Managing Editor: *Elaine Osborne*
Project Assistant: *Ed Strauss*
Text Director: *Christie Bowler*
Art Director: *Terry van Roon*
Desktop Publisher: *Andrew Jaster*

ISBN: 1-881273-99-7

1 3 5 7 9 10 8 6 4 2

Printed in the United States of America

Table of Contents

How to Use This Book

Shortly after leaving home, many teens and young adults embark on a learning curve so drastic that it resembles a roller-coaster ride. Things they never did before—such as operating a washing machine, paying bills, shopping for groceries, renting an apartment, using a credit card—suddenly become sink-or-swim survival skills. Most teens fail to learn these basics while still at home and are woefully unprepared for life in the real world when they move out on their own.

The four books in this series—*Getting Your First Credit Card*, *Buying Your First Car*, *Renting Your First Apartment*, and *Preparing For College*—were written to fill these gaps in modern education and to teach you the basic life skills you need to survive in today's jungle. In this series we walk you step-by-step through buying a used car without being conned, using a credit card without diving into debt, going to college without mortgaging your future away, and renting an apartment without headaches.

These books contain a wealth of commonsense tips. They also give sound advice from a godly, biblical perspective. It is our prayer that reading the books in this series will save you from having to learn these things in the school of hard knocks.

To get the most out of these books, you should photocopy and complete the checklists we've included. They're provided to help you take on these new tasks step-by-step and to make these books as practical as possible.

Each book contains a glossary to explain commonly used terms. If at any point while reading you need a clear definition of a certain word or term, you can look it up. Each book also contains a helpful index that allows you to find every page where a key word or subject is mentioned in the book.

CHAPTER 1

Should You Go to College?

Should You Go to College?

It's like a scene out of a scary movie. After four years of toiling away on term papers and final exams it's finally over. No more all-night, caffeine-fueled studying binges. No more half-cooked cafeteria food. This is your big day—you're graduating from college. The sun is shining. You're about to cross the stage at your graduation ceremony when suddenly the unthinkable happens. Out of nowhere a squat, rude-looking man somersaults onto the stage and blocks your way. He thrusts out his fat hand, palm up.

"Hand it over," he growls, his face so close to yours that his breath lashes out at you in short, hot gasps.

"What are you talking about?"

Before he can answer, out of the sky drops a withered, leather-clad crone dangling beneath a black silk parachute. Her feet hardly touch the stage before she springs forward and plants herself firmly before you. She hisses at the rude man.

"Back off; he's mine."

The rude man wrinkles his nose. "Forget it; I got here first!" He pushes her aside. She falls off the stage and disappears into the horrified crowd. In the confusion, you take a few steps backward, but the rude man pounces on you like a cat.

"I said, 'Hand it over,' and I won't ask again!"

"Wh–what are you talking about?" you say. "What do you want from me?"

The rude man laughs. "My money!" He grabs your arms. "I *(shake)* want *(shakes harder)* my *(turns you upside down)* money!" He drops you onto the floor.

"But I don't have your money," you say, and cower.

He takes a deep breath. "Four years and seven days ago, my lending institution granted you a loan so you could attend this fine academic institution. Today you're graduating, and

I've come to collect."

"B–b–but I don't even have a job yet. I just finished my last exam. I'm exhausted. I'm broke. I—"

"Silence!" he says. He glares out at the murmuring crowd. They grow hushed. He walks toward you with slow, lumbering steps that punctuate each word. "Thirty days from today your payments will begin—and you will make them or else!" He jabs his finger into your chest.

"Or else what?" you manage to squeak out.

"Or else this is only the beginning of a long and painful relationship. A relationship that will ruin *(he jabs your chest)* your *(jabs again)* life." He pushes you backwards. "And that's only the beginning. Wait until *she* gets through with you," he says, and gestures at the crone who is clambering back onto the stage.

"Why, w–who does she work for?" you ask.

He smiles then, and you think you almost see pity in his eyes—but only for a moment. "The government."

"Noooooooooooooooooooooooooooooooo!"

You wake up sweating and gasping for air. You look at your clock. It's 3 A.M. and you've fallen asleep at your desk. You breathe a sigh of relief. It was all a dream—or was it?

Paying for college may not be a nightmare, but next to buying a car or a house, choosing to attend college is one of the most important financial decisions you will ever make. The average cost of a four-year college degree is about $40,000, including tuition, books, room and board, and other expenses, and it's growing at a rate of about 6 to 8 percent a year. With a price tag comparable to the cost of a new luxury car, choosing to attend college is a decision that should not be taken lightly.

As someone who is considering college, you will be faced with decisions about school loans, credit cards, high book prices, pizza delivery charges, and escalating tuition costs. In order to avoid financial ruin, you need to ensure that your choices in these areas are based on sound biblical financial principles.

Answering the Big Questions

Before you consider what to study and which school to go to, you need to step back and answer some fundamental questions, such as "Who am I? What are my goals? My talents? My gifts?" Answering these questions will give you a much clearer vision of who God made you to be and what He designed you to do. Armed with this information, you will be able to make sound decisions about your future.

God didn't just mix a few ingredients in a bowl and drop you out of the sky. He made you specifically to fit the life He planned for you. He's equipped you with the perfect personality and talents so that you will excel at and enjoy what you were made to do. Finding your unique path in life is a discovery that will bring you the greatest pleasure and fulfillment in your life.

This book will take you through the following steps to help you prayerfully answer the big questions and create a plan for your future that lines up with who God made you to be.

1. Discover who you are. This is your personality, values, gifts, talents, likes and dislikes, vocational interests and skills, as well as your work priorities and values.

2. Research prospective careers that match your unique bent, interests, and abilities.

3. Set realistic vocational goals based on your research.

4. Decide which education and training opportunities will help you reach your vocational goals.

5. Develop a financial plan that will help you meet your academic and vocational goals.

6. Put your plan into action.

CHAPTER 2

Who Has God Made You to Be?

"I still can't find any of these on the course list..."

Who Has God Made You to Be?

A college career is not the answer for everyone—but God's direction is. Finding God's design for your life is much more important than just obtaining some training and then trying to find a place to use your skills and abilities. That plan usually leads straight to the back of the unemployment line. Many teenagers do not confront this issue when making decisions about postsecondary education. Looking at college as an option rather than a necessity does not mean you are throwing in the towel on your educational opportunities. It just means that you are opening yourself up to any number of different avenues down which God may lead you.

Believe it or not, most college freshmen have no idea what they are going to school for and have no ultimate goal for their lives. They're more interested in picking a favorite rock band than choosing a major. This is also true for many juniors and seniors. As a result, they may wind up changing majors once or twice during their studies, a decision that can cost upwards of $50,000 once the cost of extra tuition and the lost income from an extra year or two in school is considered.

Wasting money on training that will never be used can be avoided if you seek God's direction first. You may find it useful to walk through the following process.

Wrestle With the Purpose of Your Life

Have you begun to formulate a mission statement for your life? Have you grappled with God's purpose for creating you? These are profound, soul-searching questions that most people—adults included—struggle to understand. Easy answers to these questions are the exception rather than the rule. Yet, there is great value in the process of hammering out your personal mission statement in life.

Take time right now to prayerfully consider your purpose or mission in life; then write down what you come up with in a sentence or two. Don't just write something general like "To serve God." Be specific and concrete. Something like "To serve God by ministering to people through outdoor sports," is getting closer, but "To serve God by ministering to teenagers through rock-climbing adventure tours," is even better. This third version is the most useful to you because it states your overall purpose (to serve God), your goal (to minister to teenagers), and how you're going to reach that goal (through rock-climbing adventure tours). This statement helps you break down the path you need to take into measurable steps so you can assess how close you are to fulfilling your mission.

For example, if you want to start up a rock-climbing ministry, the first thing you need to do is learn how to rock climb. Where is the best place to learn that? Will you have to move to another city or town? But even before that, you're going to have to buy some equipment. What is the best equipment to buy? You'll have to come up with some money somehow. Once you've purchased your equipment and learned how to climb, you will need to get certified so you can lead other rock climbers. Where can you get this certification? How much will it cost? Once you get certified, how do you go about starting up a ministry? Do you link up with an organization or start something on your own or through your church? Will you need other people to help you? Where will you find them?

From this brief example, you can see how valuable it is to have your mission statement in place *before* you move forward. It helps you focus your decision making so that everything you do is purpose driven. If you make your mission statement and stick to it, you stand an excellent chance of fulfilling the goals you set out for yourself. Once you have your mission statement, hold on to it, because we will refer to it later on. You may find that it changes as you learn more about who you are and where you are going.

Take Inventory of Your God-given Talents

Psalm 139:14 states that we are "fearfully and wonderfully made" by God. Your unique God-given talents, blended with the particular people or events that have helped to shape you, provide the basis for sound career decisions. In His grace and wisdom, God provides talents that equip us to accomplish His purposes in our lives. As stewards, our responsibility is to discover our talents and use them for His glory. You can take a major step toward understanding God's purpose for your life by discovering your God-given talents.

To arrive at a well-rounded understanding of your talents, here are two primary factors you need to consider.

- *Your personality.* Some people enjoy solving relational problems, others prefer to solve problems that relate to data or ideas. Some enjoy taking the initiative in the workplace; others prefer to follow the leader. Insights into your God-given personality, your likes and dislikes, will help you to understand the kinds of work you are best suited for, which will lead to wise choices of college majors and careers.
- *Your talents.* Some people naturally work well with their hands; others work best with analytical processes. The competitive edge belongs to those who match their skill development to their natural talents.

To assist you, we've included a comprehensive career assessment that will highlight your personality strengths, vocational interests, skills, and values. Fill it out prior to reading the next chapter.

Personality Survey

PO Box 1476, Gainesville, GA 30503
(770) 534-1000

YOUR NAME: _____

DATE: _____

- Choose one of the following settings and give all your answers based on how you typically behave in that environment.

  _____ natural behavior _____ work _____ marriage/home

- Rate each line of words from left to right on a 4, 3, 2, 1 scale with **4 being most** like you and **1 being least** like you.
  You must use a different number (1, 2, 3, 4) in each column

↓	↓	↓	↓
4 Commanding	1 Enthusiastic	3 Loyal	2 Detailed

A-D	**R-I**	**O-S**	**U-C**
Commanding	Enthusiastic	Loyal	Detailed
Decisive	Expressive	Lenient	Particular
Tough-Minded	Convincing	Kind	Meticulous
Independant	Fun-Loving	Peaceful	Follow Rules
Daring	People-Oriented	Understanding	High Standards
Risk-Taker	Lively	Charitable	Serious
Courageous	Cheerful	Merciful	Precise
Confident	Inspiring	Supportive	Logical
Fearless	Good Mixer	Patient	Conscientious
Nonconforming	Talkative	Gentle	Analytical
Assertive	Popular	Even-Paced	Organized
Take Charge	Uninhibited	Good Listener	Factual
Aggressive	Vibrant	Cooperative	Accurate
Direct	Excitable	Gracious	Efficient
Frank	Influencing	Accomodating	Focused
Forceful	Animated	Agreeable	Systematic
TOTAL	**TOTAL**	**TOTAL**	**TOTAL**

Instructions:
1. **Add the numbers in each column and plot the results as shown in the example below.** The points farthest to the left and right from the Mid-Range will have the greatest influence on your personality. Note in the example graph the person is (A) Adaptive, (S) Supportive, and (C) Conscientious.
2. **Identify your profile** (those points farthest from the Mid-Range).
3. **Use those points to confirm your strengths and weaknesses listed on the next page.** Those points falling in the Mid-Range will share characteristics of both ends of the dimensions. If all points are in the Mid-Range, you are either very versatile or experiencing some sort of transition in your life and should take the survey again at another time.

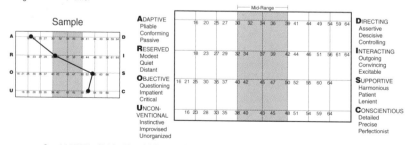

Copyright 1998 by Christian Financial Concepts, Inc. Reproduction in any form in whole or in part prohibited.

Typical Strengths and Weaknesses

The ADAPTIVE-DIRECTING dimension indicates the amount of control and decision-making authority desired.

Adaptive

STRENGTHS
1. Adapt to other's agenda
2. Cooperate
3. Move slowly into new areas
4. Be tactful
5. Focus on one thing at a time
6. Complete the current task

WEAKNESSES
1. Underestimate self
2. Not share opinions and judgments
3. Avoid taking charge
4. Not speak out
5. Be overly sensitive, internalize critisizm
6. Lack assertiveness

Directing

STRENGTHS
1. Set the agenda
2. Compete
3. Move quickly to get results
4. Be bold
5. See the global perspective
6. Take on new challenges

WEAKNESSES
1. Be a poor listener
2. Be insensitive to others
3. Be impatient, critical
4. Tend to overcommit
5. Be demanding and pushy
6. Avoid routines and details

The RESERVED-INTERACTING dimension indicates the degree of social interaction desired.

Reserved

STRENGTHS
1. Work alone or one-on-one
2. Be serious
3. Be practical
4. Not worry about what others think
5. Be modest
6. Work quietly and listen

WEAKNESSES
1. Be withdrawn, alone
2. Appear secretive
3. Be pessimistic
4. Be curt
5. Appear shy
6. Drained by social contact

Interacting

STRENGTHS
1. Meet new people
2. Be enthusiastic
3. Be optimistic
4. Make a good impression
5. Be in the limelight
6. Be talkative

WEAKNESSES
1. Avoid working alone
2. Be uninhibited
3. Be overly confident
4. Need for approval
5. Be overly involved
6. Talk too much

The OBJECTIVE-SUPPORTIVE dimension indicates the degree of harmony/stability desired.

Objective

STRENGTHS
1. Use logic over feeling
2. Be tough-minded
3. Be independent and self-reliant
4. Manage conflict
5. Be eager
6. Be dynamic

WEAKNESSES
1. Be abrupt, restless
2. Be too critical
3. Be suspicious
4. Won't compromise
5. Don't finish projects
6. Be discontent

Supportive

STRENGTHS
1. Be empathetic
2. Be warm, compassionate
3. Be supportive
4. Promote harmony
5. Be patient
6. Be even-paced

WEAKNESSES
1. Be too sensitive
2. Be naive
3. Compromise too much
4. Be afraid to confront
5. Resist change
6. Be complacent

The UNCONVENTIONAL-CONCIENTIOUS dimension indicates the degree of structure/detail desired.

Unconventional

STRENGTHS
1. Be spontaneous, unstructured
2. Be flexible, versatile
3. Be unconventional
4. Work with concepts and generalities
5. Rely on instincts
6. Take a risk

WEAKNESSES
1. Be unorganized
2. Be undisciplined
3. Be too informal
4. Overlook important details
5. Be overconfident
6. Be too reckless, careless

Concientious

STRENGTHS
1. Be organized, structural
2. Be predictable
3. Be conventional
4. Work with specifics, details
5. Research for facts
6. Take a cautious approach

WEAKNESSES
1. Be too picky
2. Be inflexible
3. Depend on rules
4. Internalize emotions
5. Be a perfectionist
6. Be overly analytical

NOTE: For more information on the DISC system, see ***Finding the Career That Fits You*** and ***Your Career in Changing Times*** by Lee Ellis and Larry Burkett, and ***Understanding How Others Misunderstand You*** by Ken Voges and Ron Braund. A more in-depth personality survey, ***Personality I.D.***, is available from Christian Financial Concepts, 1-800-722-1976, or visit their website at ***www.crown.org***.

CHAPTER 3

Matched to a Career

"Guys... I really don't think this is the best way to choose a life career!"

Matched to a Career

You don't have to talk to too many people before you realize that many of them are obviously in the wrong job. They don't know what their talents are or how to go about finding the work that God has gifted them for. As a result, they look like square pegs jammed into round holes. Few people are more miserable than those who feel trapped in an occupation they despise. When people are mismatched to their work, it's hard for them to be motivated to be excellent. They may try, but they won't do well because their hearts are not in it.

How can you avoid getting yourself into this position? By continuing the process of self-examination you began in chapter 2 and making sure your career decisions are motivated by the correct factors.

Seven Career Motivators

Job dissatisfaction has a number of causes—including uncomfortable chairs—but one of them lies in the reasons why people choose their careers in the first place. Many people choose their careers because their parents, directly or indirectly, motivate them in a certain direction. It's helpful to look at some of these motivators so you can think clearly about what is really guiding your career decisions.

1. Follow me. Many parents encourage their children to take over the family business or trade. If both of your parents are accountants, it's likely that they want you to carry on the tradition. Parents do this largely because they want their children to succeed and carry on the family legacy. But if children aren't interested in following their parents' career path, pressure to do so can lead to frustration and conflict. If you are considering following in your parents' footsteps, ask yourself, "Is it me or my parents who want me to do this?"

2. Do what I never did. Every parent wants the best for their child, especially parents who had to do without things when they were young. Perhaps your mom always wanted to be a ventriloquist but her parents could never afford a dummy. Now she may want to make sure that you don't miss out on this opportunity for fame and glory. This is a noble desire, but it can place a lot of pressure on you if your parents insist that you live out their dreams. Ask yourself, "Does the career path I'm considering really suit who I am and where I want to go, or am I just trying to please my parents?"

3. Make us proud. Parents want to be proud to tell others about what their children do for a living. Admittedly, it's a lot more exciting if your parents can tell their friends at a party that their son or daughter is a bright, up-and-coming lawyer instead of a bright, up-and-coming custodian or burger-flipper. But some parents treat their children more like trophies than people. They want their children to rise high in society so they can brag to their friends and take as much credit for the success as possible. Don't fall into this trap. As long as you are pursuing an honorable career that you feel God calling you to, you have nothing to be ashamed of.

4. Make money. Some parents will influence their children to pursue financial security above all things. This is common among "self-made" parents, or parents who were poor when they were young. While having enough money to live is important, it is only one of many factors, including one's interests and abilities, that should be considered when choosing a career. Money doesn't necessarily lead to happiness, but fulfillment in one's work does. Keep this in mind as you are researching careers.

5. Be spiritual. Many Christian parents believe that to be truly spiritual you have to go into full-time ministry. This is especially true of parents who are in the ministry and want their children to follow in their footsteps. While you should be open to the possibility that God may be calling you to full-time ministry, remember that God can minister through you no matter what occupation you choose—even professional wrestling.

6. Do what you want. Partly as a backlash against some of the other motivators we've discussed, many parents tell their children to just look at what they want to do and then go for it. This approach can lead to some exciting career choices. But keep in mind that what you want and are able to do right now may not be what you will want or be able to do in ten years. Make sure your enthusiasm is tempered with a dose of reality. For example, if you want to play professional hockey, keep in mind that of the thousands of young men who play junior hockey each year, only a fraction of those ever turn pro. And though player salaries are quite high, the average professional hockey player's career lasts only two to three years. Try and develop a plan "B"—such as going to night school during the off-season—so you will have something to fall back on after the doctor says you've taken one too many hits to the head.

7. Do what you're best at. On the surface, this sounds like a great motivation, and it is a key factor in deciding which career to pursue. But the danger arises when it is used as the sole criteria for making a career choice. What you think you're good at may not be valued in the job market. For example, you may be an excellent potter, but pottery making is not what you might call a growth industry. You may also be misreading your talents. For instance, you may be the best computer programmer in your small school, but can you compete with the best programmers in your state or country? Another problem is that you may be good at so many things that you don't know which one to pursue. (Everyone should have this problem!) While what you're best at should be a strong consideration when it comes to choosing a career path, weigh this factor against the other ones we've discussed.

Effective Career Indicators

Now that we've examined some of the unconscious motivators of career choices, it's time to look at some indicators that can help you make a choice that suits who God made you to be.

1. Your vocational interests. Make sure you do something you love. The more vocational interests you discover, the more possibilities you'll have to choose from. For this reason, it's wise to spend your high school years becoming exposed to a variety of occupational fields. This will broaden your base of interests and help you gain insights into what you really like and don't like. For example, it may be your ambition to become a writer. But as you research further into this field and discover that writing is a difficult, low-paying, often solitary profession, you may decide to choose a career related to writing, such as publishing or bookselling, that lets you be involved with books but allows for more human interaction—and a regular paycheck!

2. Your work priorities and values. Some people place a high priority on working outdoors where they can have lots of fresh air, mobility, and independence; other people value working nine-to-five in an office environment. In addition, core life values, such as achievement, recognition, financial gain, and the desire to serve God and others compete with one another in your decision-making processes. Take a moment right now to jot down the core values that influence your approach to work. (Use the form we've included.)

3. Your favorite high school subject areas. Another important clue to the selection of a career and vocational training can be found in your previous educational experiences. For instance, if you loved English, look at the job opportunities in these areas. On the other hand, if you struggled with this subject or had a hard time maintaining your interest in it, you probably don't want to pursue a degree in that field. And by the way, study hall does not qualify as a subject area.

After you have considered each of these factors, identify a few general career fields in which your personality, interests, skills, and values overlap. With some possibilities in view, determine what kind of training will prepare you for those fields. Here are some steps you can take to help you investigate potential career fields.

- Make an appointment to talk to your high school guidance counselor. He or she is an expert in helping people like you find their place in life. Your guidance counselor has access to all kinds of resources, from college catalogues and applications to personality and aptitude tests that will help you understand where you best fit in.

- Talk to your parents, friends, and other family members. They have known you for many years and will have good insights regarding who you are and what you are good at.

- Talk to college professors or high school teachers who specialize in the field you're interested in. If you don't know any professors, check out the websites for various colleges and look up professors who teach in your area. Their E-mail addresses are almost always available. Professors spend many long, lonely hours doing research and they love it when others show an interest in what they do.

- Talk to college seniors who are majoring in the subject you want to take. Don't know any? Phone your local college and ask the department head to recommend someone for you to talk to. Or ask your aunt Frieda—or your friend's aunt Frieda—who used to work in your field.

- Talk to business professionals (especially members of your church) in the career fields you are considering. If you don't know any, look up businesses in the yellow pages of your phone book and do some cold calling.
- Study professional journals and publications at your local college library.

Personality Inventory

Use the following personality inventory and career research record to record what you've learned so far about who you are and what you want to do for a career.

1. Mission statement (tentative): _____

_____

2. Personality type: _____

_____

3. Strengths: _____

_____

_____

4. Areas I need to grow in: _____

_____

_____

5. Primary talents and gifts (what I'm good at and what people have noticed I do well): _____

_____

_____

6. Secondary talents and gifts (what I'm good at but not as strong in): _____

_____

_____

7. What career I feel God calling me to: _____

_____

8. My work priorities and values (the type of environment I want to work in and what I hope to get out of my work):

_____

_____

_____

9. Things I don't want in a job or work environment:

_____

_____

10. Prospective career fields that match my interests and abilities:_____

_____

11. Future job prospects in the fields I've chosen:

_____

_____

CHAPTER 4

Different Kinds of Schools

Different Kinds of Schools

Now that you have a better handle on who you are and where you're going, it's time to determine what kind of schooling will get you there. The choices number in the thousands. They include Christian colleges, community colleges, technical schools, private colleges, and public universities. Your career plans will narrow the list dramatically, and your SATs, GPA, and finances may trim it even more. But sooner or later you will have to decide which school is best for you.

Each type of school has its own advantages and disadvantages depending on who you are and what you plan to study. The following is a brief description of the main types of schools, including some pros and cons of each.

Private or State Universities

Pros: Universities offer a broad range of courses and majors. Unlike many smaller schools, they have strong funding for staff, equipment, and other educational and recreational resources. This extra funding usually means that universities can offer a higher quality education than smaller colleges. Larger campuses also offer a diverse mix of social, professional, and religious organizations.

Cons: Large class sizes can be intimidating for some students. Also, tuition can be very expensive. According to the College Board, in 1998–99 the average cost for attending a public college or university was $10,458 per year, including tuition (about $3,800), books, room and board, and incidentals. Private college or university was over twice as expensive at $22,533 per year. Many scholarships, loans, grants, and other funding options are available (discussed more in the next chapter), but you may want to consider attending a community college for your first two years to save money.

Who Should Go? A university is for people who are planning to go into a profession—such as teaching, journalism, engineering, or computer science—that requires at least a four-year college degree. Ask your school guidance counselor to help you find out how much and what type of education is required for the career field you plan to enter.

Community Colleges

Pros: Community colleges offer many advantages that aren't available from other schools. First of all, they're much cheaper to attend than a university. Average tuition for a community college is around $1,400 per year. Compare that with the cost of attending a public or private university, and it's not difficult to see why so many students choose this option. Many students use a community college as a cost-effective "proving ground" before finishing their degree at a four-year university. At a community college they can adjust to college life, improve their grades, live at home to save money, or delay the step of declaring a major. Remember: Few employers will care where you did your first two years of college. What's important is where you graduate.

Cons: Because they operate on relatively small budgets, community colleges cannot always offer as many courses, as highly qualified professors, or as much high-tech equipment as universities. You need to weigh this factor against the money you will save by putting off attending a university for a couple of years. In education, as in most things in life, you get what you pay for.

Who Should Go? You should consider a community college if the vocation you want to pursue requires only a two-year diploma. You should also consider it if you are on a limited budget and attending a community college could help you save money by sticking closer to home for the first two years of school (that is, if your parents want you sticking around that long). Community college is also a good choice if you like smaller classes and one-on-one interaction with your professors.

Christian Colleges

Pros: Christian colleges can provide a solid education in a Christian environment presented from a Christian worldview. In addition, they offer courses and majors that aren't available at other schools, such as Christian education, youth ministry, theology, and missions.

Cons: Christian colleges are quite expensive to attend. Average tuition starts at around $7,000 per year. (That's only the tuition. Add books, room and board, incidentals and so on to that!) Some denominationally affiliated schools offer scholarships to students from their churches, and other regular funding avenues are available. You need to decide whether or not a Christian education is worth the extra expense. Also, some Christian universities offer a sheltered environment that does not adequately prepare students for the real world. If you're considering a Christian college, make sure they take a realistic, balanced approach to education which integrates and applies Christian beliefs to life in the "real world."

Who Should Go? You should consider attending a Christian college if you're interested in and can afford to get a Christian-based education. Christian college is also the natural choice if you are planning to go into full-time ministry or if you would like to pursue courses that will help you minister in your place of work later in life.

Vocational and Technical Schools

Pros: Vocational and technical schools offer diploma programs for trades, such as plumbing or carpentry, and a variety of business, industrial, and health-care professions. Students in these programs get valuable, hands-on experience, often with the help of those already working in the field. Because many of their students are already working, vo-tech schools offer flexible hours, shorter programs, and enrollments staggered throughout the year. They are particularly good at supplying you with information on the job prospects in your field before you begin your education, and they create a strong link between teaching and training by providing apprenticeships and simulated work environments.

Cons: Because of the extensive equipment requirements for many of the vocations, tuition fees can be quite expensive. Tuition for a nine-month auto mechanics course, for example, can cost up to $10,000. But this cost is balanced out by the shorter length of the course as well as the increased likelihood of employment once you graduate.

Who Should Go? Vocational or technical schools are a good choice if you want to work in a technical job that requires specific concrete skills, such as plumbing, computer systems management, nursing, carpentry, welding, or 3-D computer animation.

CHAPTER 5

Choosing the Right School for You

"Your brother has decided to go to a local college so he can still live at home and save money."

"Sigh... I was looking forward to moving into his room."

Choosing the Right School for You

Once you have decided what level of schooling to pursue and you're ready to look at individual colleges, it's time to consider what exactly you need from a school. This includes everything from tuition price to accommodation options. Use the following factors to help you evaluate each school.

Academic Competitiveness

In light of your scholastic record, do you stand a good chance of being admitted? Everyone wants to attend the best school possible, but you can waste a lot of time and money applying to schools which are out of your league. Find out the school's academic requirements, then make a realistic assessment of your abilities *before* applying. Also note that just because a school says they only accept people with a certain GPA, that doesn't always mean they won't accept people with lower marks.

Strength in Your Academic Major

Does the school excel in the area of your academic interest? Are the professors in your area well-respected in their field? Does the school have a good reputation among your prospective employers? Interview recent grads or people working in your field who are in charge of hiring new recruits. What schools make them sit up and take notice? Find businesses in the yellow pages and call their human resource managers. Or ask the college's alumni office to provide you with a list of recent grads.

Urban Versus Rural

Do you want to attend college in a city or in a rural setting? There are advantages and disadvantages to both. If you attend school in a city, you have access to all of the other things the city has to offer, such as part-time jobs in your field of study and a myriad of entertainment choices. But living in the city is expensive. And if you come from a rural area, adjusting to city life will be another stressor that you will need to manage. Rural colleges, on the other hand, offer a smaller, slower-paced environment. But you may have a harder time finding part-time work in your field than you would in the city. And you may be forced to face up to the fact that cow tipping really *is* a viable entertainment option.

Proximity to Home

How important is it for you to be close to home? Many students see college as an opportunity to finally get out from under their parents' wings. But trips home during school breaks are more expensive the farther away you are, and these need to be factored into your school budget. Some students like to be near friends and family so they pick a college that is close enough for them to drive home every weekend. Keep this factor in mind when making your choice. While getting away from your mom and dad's authority for a while may sound exciting, it may not be worth it in the long run.

Class Size

Do you thirst for anonymity and isolation? Are you the type of person who thrives in classes with hundreds of students, or will you do better in smaller classes? Smaller classes usually mean you will receive more individual attention from your professors. This is appealing for students who like to have a lot of input into their work. But if you have a more independent mindset and you don't mind just being a name on a list, you should have no trouble in larger classes.

Cost

What can you realistically afford? Everyone wants to attend the best school in their field, but thousands of dollars of debt and years of postgrad impoverishment as you pay off massive student loans is a high price to pay for an education, no matter how good it is. Try to find a compromise between your educational goals and your financial means. We will talk more about this in chapter 7.

Christian Versus Secular

Can your personal faith withstand the ultrahumanistic, politically correct bent of a secular school? This decision has to be weighed carefully by each individual. Christian colleges are usually more expensive than secular ones, but it may be worth it to you to attend a school that is built on the same foundation you are: Jesus Christ.

Accommodation

There are a number of accommodation options you can consider when going to college. Here are a few, including the pros and cons of each.

- *Student residence:* Life in residence can be a lot of fun, but it is also expensive. This factor is especially important if your budget requires that you live with your parents while attending school.

- *Apartment or house:* Renting an apartment or a house provides you with freedom and privacy. But it can also be a real trial if you get stuck with a room-mate you don't get along with or if you've moved in with a group of friends and you fool around so much that you never get any work done.

- *Room and board:* This is a very convenient situation because you don't have to worry about making meals or whose turn it is to cook each night. Everything is provided for you for one flat fee. But living in close proximity with a family does not allow for much privacy and you need to be prepared for this before going in.

Graduate Placement

What assistance does the school offer to its graduating seniors? Does it have a co-op program that allows students to "experiment" with different jobs in the workforce? This is an important factor in today's rapidly changing job market, especially if you are pursuing a career in a high-tech field. You want a school that is plugged in to industry and is constantly updating its courses to match the employment demands of the marketplace.

Tradition and Family Ties

Do you have family ties to the school? Did your parents or grandparents graduate from there? This may be a compelling reason to attend a certain college, but if the college does not suit your individual educational needs, don't be afraid to go somewhere else.

Funding Opportunities

Many schools offer entrance scholarships or grants for outstanding scholars and athletes. Scholarships are also available for students of different races or ethnic groups. Find out what each school offers and determine your eligibility. (We will discuss this further in chapter 7.)

Where can you find this information? Your high school guidance counselor is a good first place to start. Your teachers and your parents are also good sounding boards. In addition, you can check out the schools' websites (see the list of websites at the back of this book for starters). Nearly all of the information you need will be posted on-line.

School Evaluation Form

Photocopy this form and use it to record what you find out about each school you investigate.

Name of school: _____

Degrees/Diplomas available: _____

Entrance requirements: _____

_____

Cost per credit hour: _____

Hours needed to complete degree/diploma: _____

Total: _____

Average class size: _____ Co-op program? _____

Average placement percentage: _____

Graduate placement percentage: _____

Location: _____

Approximate cost of round-trip by car: _____

by bus: _____ by air: _____

Residence available? _____ Cost per year: _____

Housing list available? _____

_____

Funding opportunities: _____

_____

Jobs available on campus? _____ Type:_____

_____

Transportation options (to and from campus):_____

_____

Special clubs or groups: _____

CHAPTER 6

What Will It Cost?

"How much will college cost you?"

"I'll have to sell everything I own... and everything my parents own... and maybe everything you own too!"

What Will It Cost?

Now that you know where you're headed, it's time to figure out how much it will cost to get there. The best way to determine the real cost of going to school is to create a budget, one for school fees and one for living expenses.

Once you've chosen your short list of schools, order their course catalogues (these are usually free) and request financial information. Many schools include a sample budget in their materials. Use it to compare with the other schools. Most schools also publish a directory of people who rent apartments or provide room and board to students. If they don't, check out some ads in the local newspaper. Talk to your local pastor and see if he knows of a good church in the area. Contact churches in the area and find out if any of their members rent rooms to students. If the city or town where the college is located is not too far away, make a special trip and scout out accommodations beforehand. Photocopy the following form and use it to record your findings for each school.

Summary of Annual College Expenses

College Name: _____

SCHOOL FEES

Application Fee:	(One time payment)	$_____	Per year
Tuition:	$_____ Per credit hour	$_____	Per year
Lab Fees (If applicable):	$_____ Per semester	$_____	Per year
Registration Fee:	$_____ Per semester	$_____	Per year
Student Association Fee:	$_____ Per semester	$_____	Per year

Practicum Fee:	$_____	Per semester	$_____	Per year
Books:	$_____	Per semester	$_____	Per year
School Supplies:	$_____	Per semester	$_____	Per year
Equipment and/or Tools:	$_____	Per semester	$_____	Per year
Other_____:	$_____	Per semester	$_____	Per year
		TOTAL	$_____	**Per year**

LIVING EXPENSES

Housing

Rent:	$_____	Per month	$_____	Per year
Utilities:	$_____	Per month	$_____	Per year
Telephone:	$_____	Per month	$_____	Per year
Furniture and Appliances:	$_____	Per month	$_____	Per year
Other_____:	$_____	Per month	$_____	Per year

Food

College Meal Plan:	$_____	Per month	$_____	Per year
Groceries:	$_____	Per month	$_____	Per year
Board:	$_____	Per month	$_____	Per year

Transportation

Car Payment:	$_____	Per month	$_____	Per year
Car Insurance:	$_____	Per month	$_____	Per year
Gas and Oil:	$_____	Per month	$_____	Per year
Car Repairs:	$_____	Per month	$_____	Per year
Public Transit:	$_____	Per month	$_____	Per year
Other_____:	$_____	Per month	$_____	Per year

Other Living Expenses

Tithe: $_____ Per month $_____ Per year

Clothing: $_____ Per month $_____ Per year

Laundry: $_____ Per month $_____ Per year

Household
Supplies: $_____ Per month $_____ Per year

Personal Toiletries: $_____ Per month $_____ Per year

Entertainment: $_____ Per month $_____ Per year

Gifts: $_____ Per month $_____ Per year

Misc. Expenses: $_____ Per month $_____ Per year

Other _____: $_____ Per month $_____ Per year

Medical

Doctor: $_____ Per month $_____ Per year

Dentist: $_____ Per month $_____ Per year

Prescription: $_____ Per month $_____ Per year

Other _____: $_____ Per month $_____ Per year

TOTAL $_____ **Per year**

GRAND TOTAL
(sum of school fees and living expenses) $_____ Per year

CHAPTER 7

How Will You Pay for It?

How Will You Pay for It?

After tallying up your findings from the last chapter, you no doubt realize that paying for college is going to take some careful planning—if not a miracle! College tuitions continue to rise at a rate that is faster than inflation. One analyst predicts that in a few years the average state school, which is heavily subsidized, could cost as much as $6,000 to $8,000 per year for tuition alone. To that add room and board, books, and all the other expenses, and you may be paying $60,000 for your degree.

Because the cost of higher education has increased so dramatically during the last few years, most students and their families cannot afford to pay for college, no matter how diligently they've been saving. As a result, more people are turning to various forms of financial aid to help cover the costs. College financial assistance comes in three forms: scholarships, grants, and student loans.

Scholarships

Merit-based scholarships are awarded to students with high academic performance, artistic talent, or athletic ability. Some scholarships are provisional: If you fail to live up to the requirements, you must repay them. Other college scholarships come from private foundations and organizations: chambers of commerce, service groups, church denominations, foundations, corporations, civic clubs, alumni associations, professional associations, and trade unions.

Colleges and universities often have their own scholarships, which they use to recruit and reward superior students. Athletic scholarships get lots of attention in the press, but schools recruit academic talent too. Check with the college financial aid office for information on deadlines, eligibility, and applications for these scholarships.

Grants

Federal and state grants for college education are available to students who have a proven financial need. Like most scholarships, grant funds do not need to be repaid when you graduate. This is the closest thing to free lunch that you're ever going to get. Contact the college financial aid office for application forms and more information.

Loans

In the 1980s the federal government responded to the rising costs of higher education by making it easier for students and their families to qualify for and repay loans. They did this by offering low-interest loans of their own and offering to guarantee the loans of other institutions who lend to students.

The good news is that many more students can now afford to get a diploma or degree. The bad news is that most of those students will be in financial bondage for years after graduation while they try to pay off their loans. This means they won't be able to afford to buy a house or a car, and they may even have trouble putting food on the table.

Federally guaranteed loans essentially make Uncle Sam the cosigner on a loan made by a bank or other financial institution. If you default on the loan, it's the taxpayers who will wind up paying back the lender. Of course, the lender will still hound you to repay the loan so they can lend this money to the next student. And don't forget that your payments—or lack of them—leave a lasting mark on your credit record.

With so many loans available, it's tempting just to pay for your education with borrowed money and worry about the repayment later. Most people figure they'll be making lots of money after they graduate, and the monthly loan payments won't amount to much. And most of those folks learn that they figured wrong. An annual salary of $20,000, $30,000, or $40,000 seems like a lot of cash right now when you're flipping burgers for minimum wage. But a lot of brilliant, hardworking people in their thirties are still paying off their college loans. A recent survey found that the average student's debt load upon graduation is about $18,800. That's a 50 percent increase over the past seven years. And don't think that you'll get away with just paying the $18,800 principle. The interest charges will balloon your debt by up to 10 percent each year.

Do not underestimate the power of debt to severely hamper you from fulfilling God's will for your life. Once you've racked up the bills, you have to pay them back, even if it takes the rest of your life. The warning in Proverbs 22:7, "The rich rule over the poor, and the borrower is servant to the lender," is no idle threat. You need to seriously consider this before you plunge into debt. What if God wants you to go into missions after college; how will you be able to go if you're drowning in a sea of debt?

Alternative Funding Ideas

Over the years, people have come up with many excellent plans for getting through school without having to borrow so much money that you end up paying for your education for years to come. Here are some of them.

1. Live at home. The most economical plan is one of the most popular: Live at home, attend an inexpensive community college for one or two years, and work part-time to save up money until you can transfer to a four-year school. This may sound boring or unappealing if you were looking forward to getting away for a while. But those who carefully follow this plan graduate with the same degree as their peers, and they do so with a lot less debt to tie them down after graduation.

2. Enroll in a co-op program. In essence, this means going to school one semester and working the next. This normally adds only one year to the time it takes to earn a bachelor's degree, but it also adds approximately $8,000 a year in income. Most universities have co-op departments that will give you the details. Co-op programs can provide valuable on-the-job experience and excellent industry connections. Be careful, though; not all co-op students are successful at landing career-related jobs during their work terms. Instead of the cushy systems analyst position you were hoping for, you may wind up in shoe sales or hot dog vending. Some co-op programs have better placement percentages than others, so make sure you investigate this before you enroll.

3. Consider the military. The U.S. military offers many money-earning opportunities for college students. If you join a reserve unit in the army, navy, air force, marines, or Coast Guard, or enlist in the Air or Army National Guard, you'll be paid over $100 a month to attend a weekend drill; plus they'll drop another $190 in your lap every month you remain in school. And you pick up extra cash for training in the summer. Also, if you join the Reserve Officer's Training Corps (ROTC) unit at your college as a junior, you'll get another $100 each month and return to your reserve unit as an officer when you graduate. Contact your local recruiting office for more details.

4. Apply to the Perkins Loan program. If you plan to enter government service in the military, law enforcement, or Peace Corps, or you plan to become a teacher to students in low-income areas, consider the federal Perkins Loan program. Students who enter certain government agencies after graduation don't have to repay the loan.

5. Get a part-time job. For many college students one of the most important parts of their education takes place in the workplace as they work their way through school. Working to support yourself will give you extra incentive to do well in your classes. It also looks good on your résumé. You will need to determine how much you can work and still keep up your studies. You will also need to find a job that is flexible enough to suit your schedule.

On-campus jobs are your best bet. They are geared to fit student schedules and lifestyles. These jobs include things like working in the student information center, the library, or the campus bookstore, refereeing intramural sports, or assisting professors with administrative tasks (this job is usually only available to graduate students). Nearly every college has a job board where openings are posted. Check this out early because these jobs go fast.

The sky is the limit when it comes to off-campus job options, but you should try to find something at least remotely related to your field of study. This will help you when you are applying for your first full-time job.

In spite of all the above advice, college is about more than classes and work. There are many extracurricular activities you can get involved in, such as sports teams, Christian clubs, or the student newspaper. Make sure that your job and your studies leave you with enough time for the things that will give you a full experience of college life.

6. Take a year off to work and save money. You may be raring to get on with your education right after high school, but perhaps you should consider taking a year to work first. You will be able to save money for school, gain valuable work experience, and have time to mature and make sure that the career path you've chosen is the right one for you.

Finding a way to pay for college is complicated, but it's not impossible, so don't give up hope. Remember, with diligent effort and prayer, there *is* a way. God has a plan for your life, and you can count on Him to supply you with everything you need to carry out that plan, including money.

CHAPTER 8

Put It All Together

Put It All Together

By now you've researched your goals, the education you need to achieve them, how much your education will cost, and how you are going to pay for it. It's time to pull everything together. Use the following form to record your findings before going any further.

My Plan

Mission statement: _____

_____

The career I want to pursue: _____

_____

When I will do this (right after high school, in two years,

etc.): _____

_____

The courses and grades I need in high school: _____

_____

_____

_____

The place(s) I will study: _____

_____

What I need to major in: _____

_____

My education will cost: $_____ per year for _____ years.

TOTAL COST: $_____

My Resources

I have $_____ saved.   Total: $_____

I can earn $_____ before college starts.   Total: $_____

I can do this by:

_____

I can get a scholarship from:

_____   Total: $_____

I can get a grant from:

_____   Total: $_____

I need to apply for these by (date):

_____

I can get a job during school doing:

_____

It will pay $_____ per hour

or $_____ per year   Total: $_____

I can get other money from:

_____   Total: $_____

TOTAL RESOURCES: $_____

My shortfall or excess
(Total cost - Total resources): $_____

If everything goes as it should, you will be able to follow this plan. But just in case it doesn't, you need to build some flexibility into it so you can adapt to any unforeseen changes. For example, you might not get that scholarship you were hoping for, or you might break your leg and be unable to work the summer before school. Plan ahead so you are ready to deal with these problems as they come up.

Once you've thought everything through, the next step is to put your plan into action. Use the following checklist to make sure you remember everything.

- I have sent away to my chosen college(s) for an application form and course catalogue.
- I have filled out the application forms *completely,* included the required additional documentation and application fee, and mailed the application in on time.
- I have requested application forms for scholarships, grants, or loans.
- I have filled out the scholarship, grant, or loan application forms *completely,* included the required additional documentation, and mailed the application in on time.
- I have looked into potential housing opportunities and/or advertised for roommates.
- I have looked into potential job opportunities near the college(s) to which I've applied.

CHAPTER 9

Your First Day

Your First Day

The big day is here. You've been accepted to school. You've applied for and received your scholarship, grant, or student loan. And you may have even moved into your new place. Now what do you do?

Register

The first thing you need to do is register. This involves paying your fees, getting your student card and other documentation, and registering for your courses. Your college will let you know which day and even which hour you are to register. Be there early. The earlier you are, the more likely it is that you'll be able to get the classes you want.

If, prior to registration day, you are having trouble deciding which courses to take, consult with your faculty advisor. This person is usually the head of the department you will be studying in. He or she will help you choose the right courses so you can meet your goals and complete the requirements of your major. Haven't chosen a major yet? Don't worry. Most colleges encourage students to wait until second year to declare a major. The main thing is that you have a firm idea of the direction in which you would like to go.

Tour the Campus

This will give you a better idea of where your classes will be, where the library is, and where to find things like the gym, the student lounge, the bookstore, and the medical clinic. Virtually all colleges offer free campus tours for freshmen. They also offer things like library and computer lab orientations. Do yourself a favor and take advantage of these services. You will learn a lot of things, like how to sign up for your E-mail account, that you may not pick up on your own. It's better to learn such things *before* you are burdened with classes and assignments.

Buy Your Books

Although the sooner you get your books the sooner you can get started in your studies, it's wise to put off buying your books until classes begin. Even though campus bookstores post a list of which books are required for each course, these lists are not always accurate. Also, you may make a mistake about which class you are in, the evening class or the day class, and they might use a different text for each. You may also get to class and find out that only one of the books on the list is required and the rest are just suggested books which will only be used once or twice during the semester. If this is the case, perhaps you can make an arrangement to share a book with one of your classmates.

Another reason to put off buying books until you get to class is if you plan on purchasing your texts from the used-book store. College texts are updated almost every year, and last year's edition might not work this year. So the few dollars you saved buying used books may cause you more grief in the long run when you find out the text you bought won't do you any good. At any rate, books are always returnable within a certain time period, provided you have your receipt and the book is in the same condition in which you bought it.

Have Fun!

Freshman week at college is always full of exciting social activities that give you an opportunity to get to know your fellow class-mates. While many of these activities involve excessive drinking and other immoral behavior, there are still many events, such as barbecues or volleyball games, that can be enjoyed by everyone. Take advantage of this free time to initiate friendships and sign up for Christian clubs, such as Campus Crusade for Christ (*www.ccci.org*), the Navigators (*www.gospelcom.net/navs/*), Intervarsity Christian Fellowship (*www.gospelcom.net/iv/*), and the Fellowship of Christian Athletes (*www.gospelcom.net/fca/*), or any other organizations you want to get involved with. There will be much less time to do this once classes begin.

CHAPTER 10

Some Final Pointers

"Father, thank You that You have worked it all out for each of us... and we pray for the wisdom and everything else we will need as we begin college."

"I still can't believe I was accepted at NASA's Dental College!"

Some Final Pointers

Your college years can be one of the most exciting, stimulating periods of your life. You will form lifelong friendships, grow in knowledge, develop your skills, and mature and grow as a person and in your walk with God. But many people also meet their downfall in college and spend years afterwards trying to recover from financial, emotional, or academic disaster.

Many of the rules governing your behavior during high school no longer apply in college. No one will be standing over you and pushing you to complete your assignments on time. In college, you are expected to be responsible for managing your time and yourself wisely. There are also many diversions at college, such as football games, parties, and concerts. This massive dose of freedom can be fatal to some college careers, even to students who did really well in high school.

To ensure that you look back on your college years with fondness rather than regret, build the following habits into your life *before* you go.

Read the Bible Daily

College can be a great experience for accumulating knowledge, but only God's Word can provide true wisdom. Some of the things you will learn in college, both in and out of the classroom, will challenge your faith. By keeping your mind fixed on God and His Word, you will be able to stand firm in the face of temptation and opposition, and you will be able to keep everything in clear, eternal perspective.

Go to Church

Many students use their heavy course load, employment, or extracurricular activities as an excuse not to attend church once they get to college. Other students were forced to go to church when they were at home, but when they get out of the house, they decide to take a break and use Sunday mornings to catch up on sleep. Either way, neglecting church is a mistake. Being active in church will keep you on the right track with God and give you an eternal perspective on your studies. Find a church in your area that reaches out to college students and get involved. You may log less sleep hours, but you'll thank yourself later on.

Pray Not for Things, But for Wisdom and Courage

When God appeared to young King Solomon in a dream and asked him what he wanted the most, Solomon didn't ask for great riches or a long life, he asked for wisdom and understanding (1 Kings 3:9). God was so pleased with Solomon's reply that He not only gave him wisdom, but riches and a long life besides. Solomon became the wisest and wealthiest man on earth because he knew what was important in life. If you seek God's wisdom and direction daily, He'll guide you in the practical and material things of life.

Be Diligent

Developing good study habits and finishing assignments on time requires self-discipline, which is something you can begin working on right now. Learn how to budget your time effectively so you allow enough room for work and play. Pulling all-nighters to complete term papers or study for tests seems like a rite of passage for most college students. But caffeine addiction and bloodshot eyes can be avoided if you plan ahead. Remember, you are paying for your education; that makes you a consumer. Get the most for your money by putting your best effort into your studies.

Learn to Budget

If you can learn to budget while at home, you will have it made by the time you get to college. Use the tools in this book to help you do this. The key to successful budgeting is to always live *below* your means; always spend less than you make. That sounds elementary, but you would be amazed by how many people borrow to live far beyond their means, then borrow more to pay back the previous month's borrowing. Plan your spending, pay your bills on time, and you should never have a problem.

Learning to budget includes learning how to use credit cards. Despite their name, credit cards should never be used for credit. Use them as a substitute for cash, and then pay them off at the end of each month. The first month you cannot pay off your credit card, destroy it. If you don't follow this advice, the high interest rate you will pay on the money you borrow will quickly drain your financial resources.

Be a Good Tenant

If you move away from home to go to college, you'll likely end up sharing accommodations with someone else. Whether you're in a college dorm, a house, or your own apartment, you will need to learn how to get along with other people. These other people include your landlord or landlady and/or your roommate(s). Living in close quarters with others, such as a dorm situation, creates many possibilities for conflict. Take time now to learn how to follow the rules of the house, pay the rent on time, play your music quietly, keep foul odors to a minimum, and clean up after yourself. Live as you would at home—or better. (For more on this topic, see another book in this series, *Renting Your First Apartment*.)

Countless friendships have been damaged because people neglected to learn and apply these simple skills before moving in with each other. Roommates who start out as good friends before college wind up enemies by the end of the year because they haven't learned how to resolve simple issues like how to divide up the household chores. Do yourself and your roommate(s) a favor and get on top of issues right away. If everyone is doing his or her part and the communication lines are open, everything should go fine.

By trusting in God and following His principles both while you prepare for college and when you are there, your college years will be an academic and spiritual success. Just remember to follow these three simple steps:

- Plan ahead.

- Prayerfully consider each step.

- Commit everything you do to the Lord.

Websites

The World Wide Web is one of the most effective research tools for finding information on colleges and financial aid resources. You can visit the websites of individual schools, find and compare scholarships, or use sample budgeting programs to work out your financial plans.

CAREER GUIDANCE

For more information on how to choose a career and plan your education, go to the website for Christian Financial Concepts *(www.crown.org/lifepathways/index.htm)* and inquire about their Life Pathways program, or call them at 770-534-1000.

UNIVERSITIES AND COLLEGES

Every Internet search engine or directory has a category for education. This is a great place to look for information on all types of colleges and schools. Here are some of the major search engines.

www.altavista.com

www.looksmart.com

www.excite.com

www.hotbot.com

www.infoseek.com

www.lycos.com

www.yahoo.com

FINANCIAL AID

www.collegeboard.com
Here you can locate scholarships, loans, internships, and other financial aid programs from noncollege sources that match your education level, talents, and background. Once you complete the electronic form, their search engine will find potential scholarships from a database of over one million awards.

www.collegeispossible.org
This site will show you how to find the books, websites, and other resources that admissions and financial aid professionals consider most helpful. It also includes a brief look at student financial aid programs, basic facts about college prices and student aid, and myths and realities about paying for college.

www.embark.com
This site will help you choose the right school, apply on-line or acquire an application form, and find out about grants, scholarships, and loans that you may qualify for. It even provides you with advice and information that will help you when you're at school.

www.estudentloan.com
This site will help you find and compare various student loan programs. It also includes on-line applications for many of the loans.

www.fafsa.ed.gov
This an official site of the U. S. Department of Education which features an on-line form that you may use to file a Free Application for Federal Student Aid (FAFSA).

www.fastweb.com
This site bills itself as the Internet's largest free scholarship search with a database of over 400,000 scholarships. It features information on local and federal aid, work-study, and grant programs.

www.finaid.org

This is a comprehensive free resource for student financial aid information on the Web. It features a free scholarship search, financial aid calculators, a glossary, and a bibliography of helpful books.

www.kaplan.com:8000/miniapps/tuition/index.html

If you want a humorous break from the serious business of financial aid, take a whirl at "Tuition: Impossible." In this web-based game, your mission is to earn, save, and manage enough money to pay for college while navigating through a number of real-life (and wacky) scenarios. Play wisely, and you'll have enough money for tuition, books, *and* late-night pizza.

www.theoldschool.org

This website features information on and access to federal financial aid resources, general financial aid resources, loans and lenders, scholarship search services, and state agencies and assistance.

Glossary

Apprenticeship: A program that enables someone to learn a trade or business "on-the-job" or in a simulated work setting.

Budget: A written plan that details your income and expenses for the year, month, or week. It is a tool that allows you to plan how you will save, spend, and earn your money.

Co-op program: A work-study program that allows college students to attend school one semester then work the next.

Degree: The certificate you receive upon completion of the requirements of your university major.

Diploma: The certificate you receive upon completion of the requirements of your one- or two-year college major.

Grant: Financial aid offered to students by colleges, businesses, and nonprofit organizations. Grants do not have to be repaid, and they are usually given to students based on their financial need.

Major: Your core area of study in college.

Mission statement: A short, specific summary of your purpose in life and how you will achieve it.

Residence: Student housing provided by universities or colleges.

Room and board: An accommodation situation where the tenant pays a monthly lump sum for his or her meals and a room.

Scholarship: Financial aid for education offered to students by colleges, businesses, or nonprofit organizations. Scholarships cover all or part of a student's tuition and do not have to be repaid. They are usually granted based on academic or athletic achievement.

Student loan: Loans for students that are guaranteed by the federal or state government. These loans are interest free while students attend school full-time, but must eventually be repaid.

Tenant: Someone who rents a house or apartment.

Tuition: The basic cost for attending college. Tuition only covers the cost of your courses; books and other materials are extra.

Vocation: A profession or occupation, such as teaching, carpentry, or architecture.

Index

Larry Burkett's Stewardship for the Family™ provides the practical tips and tools that children and parents need to understand biblical principles of stewardship. Its goal is *"Teaching Kids to Manage God's Gifts—Time, Talents and Treasures."* Stewardship for the Family™ materials are adapted from the works of best-selling author on business and personal finances, **Larry Burkett**. Larry is the author of more than 60 books and hosts the radio programs "Money Matters" and "How to Manage Your Money," aired on more than 1,100 outlets worldwide. Visit Larry's website at www.mm4kids.org